THE
ELOQUENT BATON

THE
ELOQUENT BATON

by

WILL EARHART

M. WITMARK & SONS

EDUCATIONAL PUBLICATIONS

New York

FOREWORD

This book is not an exhaustive treatise on conducting. More modestly it limits itself to discussing solely the principal feature of that technique by which a conductor expresses himself, namely, his use of the baton. That use has been beautifully illustrated by far more able musicians and conductors than I; but on the other hand most accounts of what such conductors do are very incomplete. Their administrative and metronomic functions have been adequately described, but the many sensitive modifications of their beat by which they invest it with varied expressive qualities have not been similarly treated.

Much more than even an expressive technique of the baton goes, of course, to the making of a conductor. A conductor must know music broadly, deeply. Its theory, its forms, its history, its instrumentalities of expression, as they were and as they are, its literature, the traditions of its interpretation, must all be known to him—at least within the limits of his practice. He must also have become something of an æsthetician; must know what effects are produced by various factors, dynamic, rhythmic, harmonic, coloristic and formal, and be psychologically adept in their use. Moreover, he must certainly be an artist, possessed of a warmth and fineness of feeling with respect to music that is at least greater than that of the performers under him, or than that possessed by the majority of those who constitute his audiences. And he should be an impressive personality, having more than musical power only, to the end that he will not be utterly without interest and charm and strength to his constituents in the moments when his baton is not waving over them. Sincerity and honesty of character and a manner and method that make it a pleasant task to work with him in rehearsals, perhaps complete the list of his desirable qualifications.

But if all this be necessary, one book, however large, could contribute only infinitesimally to the making of a conductor. Teachers of music by the dozen, textbooks and other books on music by the hundred, hours, days, and years of study, observation and experience, life itself in rich and wide play, must all bear their part. To make a conductor is a complex, not a simple thing.

However, after a conductor is potentially made, it may be possible to say something in a little book like this that will help him to express himself well through the established forms of conductorial practice. Like expressive playing on piano or violin, expressive conducting has its correlated technique, and this technique can be observed, described and taught. To observe, describe and teach those forms, then, especially with respect to their expressional features, is the purpose of this book.

The book would in all probability never have been written had not the author been urged to the task by students and professional associates who have received or observed his teachings. It is his earnest hope that their expectations with respect to its usefulness may not be disappointed.

Acknowledgments

The excerpts from *Tubal Cain* by Harvey B. Gaul, used as musical illustrations in the text, are reprinted by kind permission of C. C. Birchard & Company, Boston, Mass., owners of the copyright. Excerpts from *The Swan and the Skylark* by Goring-Thomas are reprinted by kind permission of Boosey and Co., Inc., owners of the copyright.

CONTENTS

THE
ELOQUENT BATON

CHAPTER ONE

Direction in General

1. Among other properties beats have *direction*. For several reasons this property deserves first attention.

2. Direction is the *form* of the beat. All other properties are shades of quality that may be poured into that form.

3. The form is essential because it is laid upon the very measure-structure of the music itself and faithfully reflects it.

4. The form of beat that best outlines the rhythmic truth for each kind of measure has become quite well standardized. Lack of knowledge and technique in connection with it seems to imply ignorance of conducting and obtuse sensibilities with respect to measure-architecture. In addition, all musicians experienced in ensemble playing rightly expect this form of beat because it is expository of measure-structure to them: and they have great difficulty in playing correctly and beautifully under a heterodox beat that, in comparison, ignores basic rhythmic facts.

5. The 1st beat in a measure is normally a moment of strength. The composer knew it was a 1st beat, and put a bar in front of it when he wrote his music, only because it spoke a stronger language. He found that the harmony changed, or a longer note insisted on attention, or a bit of musical pattern began, and said "accent."

6. The 1st beat for a measure is always a *down* beat; for one can strike with power, emphasis, energy, only down. Gestures of energy, such as striking the fist into the hand or stamping the foot, tend to take a downward direction. The downward

1

inflection of the voice also has an air of decision, finality. **One** does not say "Halt" with an upward inflection.

7. The down beat, however greatly its power is modified or lessened, should always be clearly distinguishable *as* the 1st beat in a measure. Chorus conductors are often careless about this matter because each singer in the group sees the notation for all that the other singers and the accompanist do, and consequently can hardly lose the place. But an orchestra player, say a trombonist, may have twenty-seven measures of rest, during which the other instruments play *accelerando, ritardando,* etc.: and he has no clue to the passing of those measures (save a keen musical instinct) except the sketches of them described by the baton of the conductor. It is accordingly the latter's duty to make those sketches clear: but while doing this he need in no degree lessen the artistry of his conducting.

8. The remaining beats in a measure are similarly designed to indicate the relative weight or emphasis of the rhythmic moments they signalize: and they are further determined by the necessity of adapting themselves to convenient forms of our physiological action. Perhaps the principal requirement in this action is that successive movements be, as far as possible, in different and balancing directions—a down beat in a 2-beat measure being balanced by an up beat.

9. As the 1st beat in every measure must be *down*, the *last* beat in every measure *must be up*, so that the baton will be in right position for the ensuing measure.

10. Before diagramming the beats and making explanatory comments it will be well to prepare the way for a better understanding by stating a point of view from which the explanations take their rise and upon which they depend. It is this: *A beat is not a duration but a point in time*. Thus a metro-

nome or the ticking of a clock marks beats by clicks that need have no duration whatever except enough to make them audible. They may be of the briefest conceivable duration without impairing the fact of pulsation. It follows that the movement of a baton is largely *a movement between beats* or *a movement that terminates in a beat;* and it is followed by another movement that similarly terminates in another beat. *What happens between beats* (to the baton) *is therefore of greater musical significance than the making of the beat itself;* and it is *the direction described by these movements between beats that impresses the eye as being the direction of the beats themselves.*

CHAPTER TWO

The Two-Beat Measure

The beats for the various measures, as ordinarily sketched, may now be shown: but as the conventional sketches are far from delineating the whole truth, each will be presented separately and will immediately be supplemented by many modifying comments.

I

The TWO-BEAT measure (2/2, 2/4, 2/8) is beaten as a *Down*-up. Imperfectly diagrammed the beat is:

The arrow-head shows the point of the <u>ictus</u> or <u>stroke of the beat</u>—the point where the culmination, or termination, or arresting of the movement, marks out the moment that is the beat itself.

The diagram is imperfect because:

1. It is impossible to show what is meant; namely, that the up-stroke traverses the same line as the down-stroke, but in reverse direction.

2. The arrow-head of the 2nd beat is at the top of the up-stroke, implying that the culmination of the stroke—the real beat—is made there, and in an upward direction; and this is contrary to the truth, except on rare occasions and then only in a very general and partial way.

What really happens can not be stated in a word or outlined in one sketch. *Tempo, Phrasing,* and what, for want of a better word, must be termed *Style* or *Kind of Expression,* all affect the beat.

II

Remembering that so far as a beat must be decisively struck at all it is struck downward, we will start with:

as a more accurate representation of the path traversed.*

1. The diagram is that of a beat appropriate to music *in slow or moderate tempo* and somewhat *marcato* (as contrasted with *legato*) style. E.g., it would be applicable in the following:

---

* The stroke will be indicated throughout in these graphs by an unbroken line; the movement between beats, or by which the baton reaches position for the next stroke, by a dotted line.

OLAV TRYGVASON, *Grieg*, Op. 50

Even in this brief musical excerpt the energy and decisiveness of the 2nd beat is not quite uniform in all measures. Where it is greatest, as indicated by the accent marks in the accompaniment, the hand would *rise higher* in preparation for the 2nd beat—THOUGH NEVER SO HIGH AS FOR THE 1ST BEAT—and strike downward further, *approximately to the spot reached by the 1st beat.*

2. As the tempo is increased or the style, regardless of tempo, made more flowing, the beat is modified by innumerable delicate gradations. Many of these are not connected with direction, but those that are so connected will be treated now. E.g.,

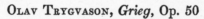

This beat is more appropriate to another excerpt from *Olav Trygvason* which occurs a little later in the same movement, and is as follows:

OLAV TRYGVASON, *Grieg*, Op. 50

Again the 2nd beat is not uniform in all the measures. From

the fifth measure on, the accent in the accompaniment on the 2nd beats will obviously require more decisive punctuation.

3. If the movement is extremely flowing, any very vigorous stroke on the 2nd beat—and, indeed, on the 1st beat—disappears. In this case the *forearm* WAVES the baton, so to speak, and the wrist PUNCTUATES *the flowing movement* by a more or less decisive dipping, like that described by the wrist when one wig-wags a signal with a handkerchief. The motion will be most quickly grasped if the baton is first waved through this sort of figure:

From the first a tendency will be felt to mark out beat-moments within this flow by flexings of the wrist. With this wrist-motion added the movement may be represented somewhat like this:

Such smooth flow, lightly punctuated, would be appropriate in the following:

Softly Now the Light of Day, adapted from *von Weber*

As in all music, the measures in the example are not uniform. If beaten uniformly—and if the singers rightly obey the beat—only monotony results. The modifications of beat that result in expressive variety involve many properties other than direction, but we shall consider only sharpness of stroke now.

(a) In the first two measures the quietness of the harmony makes all beats almost uniform. The beat is hardly more than a gentle waving of the baton over this figure:

If loss of precision in attack on the part of the choir began to be manifest, the beat would have to be sharpened, of course, as shown in the sketch immediately preceding the musical example.

(b) The phrase reaches its crest at the beginning of meas. 3, and here a diminished-seventh (dissonant) chord lends intensity. The down-stroke at this point would accordingly be slightly more marked. The "up"-beat, too, in this measure, would receive slightly sharper definition—certainly more than the "up"-beat in the next measure, which comes in the middle of a half-note.

(c) The necessity for clarity, clear-cut delineation, increases in proportion to the novelty, strangeness or complexity of that which the ear has to grasp. The conductor will feel that the two beats for the modulatory chords in meas. 6 must be given clear definition by means of decisive (though not heavy) wrist strokes. The 1st beat in meas. 7, as climax of the phrase and goal of the modulatory chord preceding, must also be decisive.

(d) The third phrase should be given more emphasis because it must advance beyond the point of vapid repetition of the first. Other properties than the outline of the beat traversed should be, and quite naturally will be, employed: but a sharpening of the angles of the beat toward the types described in II-1-2 above will be found appropriate.

(e) In the last four measures, and especially in the first three beats of these, there is a noticeable increase in intensity. The beat here accordingly becomes decisively marked, approaching the outline of that described in II-1; and then it gradually subsides.

4. When the tempo is very rapid anything like a definite stroke on the 2nd beat, even with the wrist, is likely to disappear, and the up-beat becomes a mere return to the position from which the down-beat started. Such a return, however, is in time. There is little or none of an up-*stroke*, but the hand or baton reaches the end of the "straight-up" movement and is *arrested* at the moment of the 2nd beat. In moving up the baton traverses the line made by the down-beat, and this, of course, can not be depicted. The movement may be suggested, however, by this sketch:

(a) The beat described would serve well for much of Mozart's Overture, *Die Entführung aus dem Serail*, for instance at the opening, which is as follows:

OVERTURE: DIE ENTFÜHRUNG AUS DEM SERAIL, *Mozart*

(b) But later in the movement the 2nd beat many times has greater intensity or weight, e.g., in the following:

OVERTURE: DIE ENTFÜHRUNG AUS DEM SERAIL, *Mozart*

Without doubt the 2nd beat, as energetic syncopation, should here be given greater strength by the conductor than the 1st beat, resulting in a movement somewhat of this pattern:

(c) Between the slighting of the 2nd beat, as in (a) above, and the slighting of the 1st beat, as just described in (b), are gradations that meet in equality of the two beats. Thus, toward the end of the same overture, about half the strength of the orchestra strikes the 1st beat of the measure *sf*, and the other half replies with the 2nd beat *sf*. At the extremely rapid tempo very great weight can not be put on two beats in succession: but a 1st beat as in (a) above, and a 2nd beat as in (b) can be approximated. The *sf* on the 1st beat will be given by the players with less encouragement from the conductor, of course, than that on the 2nd beat.

5. In the *most rapid tempi*, in 2-beat measure, the 2nd beat really does disappear as a distinct pulsation. The most familiar example, as well as the best, is probably the first movement of Beethoven's *Fifth Symphony*. There is but one beat to a measure in that movement: the 2nd beat is not felt at all. The return of the hand to the starting position is therefore unnoticed, undefined, negligible. One of the greatest orchestra conductors in the United States, in order to avoid the consequent monotony and emptiness of a straight "down-up," long continued, habitually beats the measures in pairs, like a letter U, described first from left to right (DOWN-up), then from right to left (DOWN-up), the complete U in either direction being a measure.

SYMPHONY No. 5, *Beethoven*

CHAPTER THREE

The Three-Beat Measure

I

The THREE-BEAT measure (3/2, 3/4, 3/8) is beaten *Down-right-up*. Imperfectly diagrammed the beat is

Almost all statements made in the preceding chapters, DIRECTION IN GENERAL and THE TWO-BEAT MEASURE, apply to this 3-beat movement. In particular the reader should recall that *the movement that occurs between beats is important and is what gives the sense of direction:* and that the actual *beat-stroke*, so far as it is decisively made, approximates a downward direction.

II

An energetic and sharply marked ONE-*two-three*, such as is suggested by the foregoing imperfect diagram, is more accurately delineated thus:

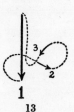

or, if broader, thus:

1. The down-beat should be made to swing a little to the left, so that the next motion, to the right, will *reverse the movement*. (See Chapter One, Par. 8.)

2. The two diagrams are of beats that might both be employed in conducting a chorus through *America*. The first of the two would be appropriate at the beginning, where energy and decision, with buoyancy, were components of the style. If the ending were then taken very broadly, as under the technical term *allargando*, the second form of beat would be appropriate.

3. As the tempo of a 3-beat measure is increased, or as the style becomes more *legato*, the beat, through innumerable gradations, is greatly modified.

(a) In particular the 2nd beat is made *shorter*, becomes less *downward* in direction, and, since a genuine *stroke* is characteristically down, derives definition as much from decisive *arrest* of motion as from a definitely propelled stroke. Such a beat, which might be diagrammed

would be appropriate to the following introductory strain:

Symphony in B Minor (Unfinished), *Schubert*

(b) Further on in the same movement the passage following, full of rugged energy, occurs. No conductor who feels the mood can escape conducting it, especially the second measure quoted, with a decisive ONE, two, three, substantially of the outline given in II (this chapter), preceding.

SYMPHONY IN B MINOR (UNFINISHED), *Schubert*

4. If the movement is quite quick and flowing the 2nd and 3rd beats become even less decisively marked than in II-3 (a) above, somewhat as indicated in this figure:

Arrest of motion alone here marks the 2nd and 3rd beats. Such a figure might well be employed in conducting parts of the first movement of Beethoven's *Eroica* symphony, as in the example below:

SYMPHONY No. 3 (EROICA) *Beethoven*

5. At still faster *tempo*, and with still less emphasis attached to the 2nd and 3rd beats, the 2nd beat becomes shorter and more upward in direction. The effect, in various gradations significant of varying *tempi* and degrees of emphasis upon the later beats, may be outlined thus:

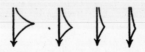

These forms would be appropriate to the following excerpt:

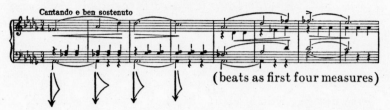

(beats as first four measures)

6. One type of very rapid triple measure, in which the 3rd beat has value because it begins the phrase, changes melody-note or harmony, or has other distinction, is perhaps best beaten by a vertical *"Down-up,"*

But in this case the up-beat is made at the moment of the 3rd beat, and does not divide the length of the measure equally with the Down-beat, as would be the case in a 2/4. Such a beat would be applicable to a selection such as the following:

INVITATION TO THE DANCE, *von Weber*

The 2nd beat in these measures has negligible weight, but the strength imparted to the 3rd beat requires that it receive decisive recognition.

7. If there is but one clear *beat-moment* in a triple measure, namely, the **"Down,"** *the form of Down-up shown in the pre-*

ceding paragraph applies, except that the return to the top of the stroke is not necessarily (or perhaps *possibly*) *made at a definite division of the measure* (the 3rd beat) but is free. The conductor, in short, feels and responds only to a "Down." Such beat would naturally be used for the passage quoted next (the Finale from Grieg's *Olav Trygvason,* Op. 50), in which, at a tempo now accelerated above the M.M. $\d = 112$ which began the movement, a measure entire is but one brief beat.

Olav Trygvason, *Grieg*

CHAPTER FOUR

The Four-Beat Measure

I

The FOUR-BEAT measure (4/2, 4/4, 4/8) is beaten DOWN-left-*right*-up. An imperfect diagram that suggests the real movement is

but here again the stroke, in so far as there *is* any decisive *stroke*, is indicated wrongly, as being otherwise than *down*, and no intimation is given of the various inflections necessary in differing *tempi* and styles, or of the movements that articulate one stroke with another.

II

In connection with the 4-beat measure it is necessary to discuss Simple and Compound measures. The discussion involves, to an extent, PHRASING : but a fuller discussion of that subject must be deferred to the separate chapter under that title.

1. A 4-beat measure ordinarily contains one strongly accented beat, the ONE, or DOWN, and one beat, the *three* or *right*, that receives a lesser accent. These are usually termed, respectively, the *principal* and the *subordinate* accent. The long

sweep to the *right*, in the diagram of the 4-beat movement,
recognizes the strength of the 3rd beat, as compared with that
of the 2nd or that of the 4th beat.

2. If the *3rd* beat (the subordinate accent) were equal in
strength to the 1st beat (the principal accent), there would be
no 4-beat measure (or rhythmic unit) but we should have, in
place of it, only *two measures of two beats each.*

3. Two measures of 2/4 might therefore be figured as
$\searrow \underset{1}{\quad} \underset{2}{\quad}$, $\searrow \underset{1}{\quad} \underset{2}{\quad}$: but one measure of 4/4 would then be comparatively figured as $\searrow \underset{1}{\quad} \underset{2}{\quad} \searrow \underset{3}{\quad} \underset{4}{\quad}$.

4. But the question arises whether there may not be, com-
parably to the Duple rhythm and the Triple rhythm discussed
in Chapters Two and Three, a *genuine Quadruple rhythm*, that
could be correctly figured only as $\searrow \underset{1}{\quad} \underset{2}{\quad} \underset{3}{\quad} \underset{4}{\quad}$.

5. The truth is that every shade of accentual gradation may
be found in 4-beat measures, from $\searrow \underset{1}{\quad} \underset{2}{\quad} \searrow \underset{3}{\quad} \underset{4}{\quad}$ (which is really
two 2-beat measures printed together), to $\searrow \underset{1}{\quad} \underset{2}{\quad} \underset{3}{\quad} \underset{4}{\quad}$, which
indicates a real Quadruple rhythm: and all of these sensitive
gradations may appear in various portions of a single extended
composition. If this were not so, music would be comparatively
monotonous—would not have the infinite, sensitive variety that
it possesses.

6. A composition in 4/4 may thus contain measures that, by
reason of the strength or superior interest attaching to the 3rd
beat as printed, are really two measures of 2/4. Conversely, *a
composition in 2/4 may contain passages that, because of lack
of interest or strength attaching to each alternate accented
beat, are really passages in 4/4, divided by twice too many
bars.* For illustration, the reader should study the passages following, and observe how his feeling varies with respect to the
degree of emphasis appropriate to the alternate accented beats.

Hymn of Praise, *Mendelssohn*

The Crusaders, *Gade*

THE SWAN AND THE SKYLARK, *Goring-Thomas*

7. Varying degrees of emphasis upon the 3rd beat require various modifications in the outlines that are to be presented of the baton's movement for 4-beat measures. Still more extensive modifications (later to be analyzed) in other properties that the beat possesses are, of course, required.

III

1. More accurate than the conventional diagram given at the beginning of this chapter is the following outline of movement appropriate to what may be considered the normal or ordinary rhythm of a 4-beat measure:

In accordance with the factor of *reversal of direction* from beat to beat, the down-beat now swings a little to the right instead of, as in the 3-beat measure, to the left. Blunders in the direction of the 2nd beat (as between 3/ and 4/) on the part of the unskilled, may often be avoided by fastening attention on this slight deflection of the down-beat from the perpendicular: to the *left* in 3/, to the *right* in 4/.

The "normal" beat shown would be appropriate to the following opening measures:

Iphigenia in Aulis, *Gluck-Wagner*

BASSOONS I-II-III

VIOLIN I

VIOLIN II

VIOLA

2. If the beats are all very emphatic (*marcato*) the result, as always, is that *all strike almost the point in space struck by "One,"* and that the direction of each stroke is more determinedly downward. The movement is difficult to decipher, when outlined, but is much as follows:

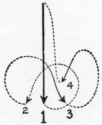

(The student should place some small object, about the area of a luncheon plate, at the point struck by the down-beat, and note that in beating a *marcato* "One-Two-Three-Four," *all* the beats will *actually strike* the object.)

This *marcato* beat would be nicely applicable to the excerpt from Mendelssohn's *Hymn of Praise* quoted on page 22.

3. In 4/-measures that approximate the rhythm of two 2/'s the 2nd and 4th beats take a more lateral direction. The form then is approximately and might properly be applied in the following excerpt:

SIGURD JORSALFAR, *Grieg*

4. If a genuine Quadruple rhythm is approximated, *all* the beats following the Down-beat tend toward a lateral movement and toward indication by wrist-movement or arrest of motion. Further, since the accents are in such case widely separated, the measures being long, the Down-beat is likely to be more than ordinarily emphasized. It becomes, so to speak, an initial impulse which must carry the mind over a long stretch of unmarked territory. The movements that reflect this form are somewhat as follows:

The excerpt from A. Goring Thomas' *The Swan and the Skylark*, quoted earlier in this chapter, provides an excellent example of music for which this beat would be suitable.

5. Faster measures, if *legato*, retain practically the form shown in Par. 4; if *marcato*, the form shown in Par. 2. If, however, the rhythm of two 2/'s occurs in very rapid tempo, as for instance an *accelerando ending*, a beat is likely to result that has approximately this form:

Indeed, the figure,

might well suggest the movement, since the 3rd beat merely *retraces the path* of the 2nd (though with a vigorous *stroke* instead of a glide), and the 4th beat retraces the path of the 1st, but with a *glide* instead of a stroke. Such movement will often be found the most suitable one for an entire composition, particularly in the case of very rapid 4/4 marches in which only the 1st and 3rd beats are rhythmically strong. The *March* from *Tannhäuser* and the chorus *With Sheathed Swords*, from *Damascus*, by Costa, are examples. More often, in an *accelerando*, the movement gradually supplants four more equally balanced strokes, like those shown earlier, as, for instance, in progressing through the following excerpt from Grieg's *Olav Trygvason:*

Olav Trygvason, *Grieg*

Olav Trygvason, *Grieg* (continued)

CHAPTER FIVE

The Six-Beat Measure

I

1. The directions in SIX-BEAT measure may be more easily outlined than described in words. One form of beat that is much followed is suggested by the following diagram:

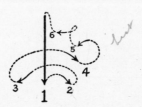

The movement might be described as DOWN-right-left-*right*-up-up, but both lines and words are inaccurate in so far as they ignore the downward inflection that, as we have observed, is given all decisive strokes.

2. Another form of 6/4-beat that is supported by many excellent authorities is:

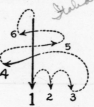

It is an excellent form, except for the fact that the 4th beat, because of its upward direction, lacks weight. It is true that it can be struck downward and then be carried up, but the carry is somewhat prolonged compared with that required in connection with the first form given.

3. Still another form sometimes followed is:

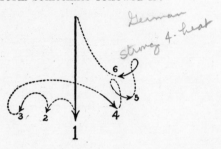

It can not be recommended, because it does not delineate the true rhythm, the 6th beat being altogether out of proportion.

II

1. Just as a 4-beat measure is usually, if not always, a compound of two duple rhythms, so a 6-beat measure is usually, if not always, a compound of two triple rhythms. That is, a 6-beat measure ordinarily contains just two accented beats: the ONE, or DOWN (principal accent) and the *four* or *right* (subordinate accent).

2. The interest or energy of the subordinate accent (the 4th beat) varies greatly, ranging from equality with the 1st beat to a level indistinguishable from the unaccented beats. A composition in 6/ may therefore contain measures that range from $\searrow$ — — $\searrow$ — — (which is actually two meas-
1 2 3 4 5 6
ures of 3/ *with every other bar left out*), through $\searrow$ — — $\searrow$ — —,
1 2 3 4 5 6
and $\searrow$ — — $\searrow$ — —, and $\searrow$ — — $\searrow$ — —, to $\searrow$ — — — — —.
1 2 3 4 5 6   1 2 3 4 5 6   1 2 3 4 5 6
Conversely, compositions in 3/ may contain passages in which no particular interest or energy distinguishes the 1st beat in each alternate measure: and such passages are actually, there-

fore, in 6/, *twice too many bars* being inserted. The excerpts
following, in 6/ and 3/, will illustrate these sensitive gradations
of accent.

STILL AS THE NIGHT, *Bohm*

STILL AS THE NIGHT, *Bohm*

THINE EYES SO BLUE AND TENDER, *Lassen*

SYMPHONY IN E FLAT, *Mozart*

INVITATION TO THE DANCE, *von Weber*

INVITATION TO THE DANCE, *von Weber*

3. The movements of the baton in 6/-measures must reflect these varying degrees of strength with respect to subordinate accents. The figures and comments following are planned accordingly.

III

1. Six beats are used characteristically in 6/2 (which is comparatively rare) or in 6/4. In 6/8 the tempo of eighth-notes is usually so rapid that *only two beats per measure are required.* A slow 6/8 measure is, however, *identical in rhythm, character and conductorial beat with a 6/4 measure.*

2. Assuming the normal 6/4 measure, or slow 6/8 measure, to be such as would be correctly represented by ＼＿＿＼＿＿, the appropriate movement may be outlined as

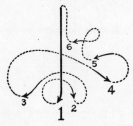

Note that the Down-beat veers slightly to the left, in preparation for the reversal of direction to the right, and that similar preparation for reversal of direction attends all the other strokes. The 4th beat, because of its strength as an accented beat, is lifted to a higher point, and is longer. This beat would well indicate the quality of the following excerpt:

THINE EYES SO BLUE AND TENDER, *Lassen*

3. If the beats are more emphatic than the normal, and especially if they are also slow, they will, as is usual in such cases, *concentrate more closely on the point struck by the* ONE, and be still more definitely downward in direction. The lines that delineate this movement run together confusingly, but an effort to trace them in the following figure will not be without value:

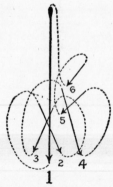

Such a beat would be appropriate to the music following:

Nazareth, *Gounod*

4. If the tempo is faster and the strokes less emphatic than the normal shown in Par. 2, above, the beat will tend to spread and closely approximate the figure given in the first paragraph of this chapter. In this case, *as in all cases where the beat spreads laterally*, there is really no *stroke* on the lateral motions, but rather a mere *arrest* of motion, decisive and significant, at the beat-moment. If we indicate this arrest by a solid black line instead of an arrow-head, the effect may be well suggested thus:

The following excerpt would be satisfactorily beaten so:

Symphony in G Minor, *Mozart*

	Andante
Horns in E flat	
Violin I	
Violin II	
Viola	
Cello and Bass	

(*Continued on next page.*)

SYMPHONY IN G MINOR, *Mozart* (continued)

5. Occasionally a composition in 6/8 presents a tempo or style that is too rapid for six beats (which would make it "busy" or "fussy") and yet too slow for two beats (which would let it "die" between beats). A beat that is substantially Down—down, up—up, may be advantageously employed for such pieces. Its outline is:

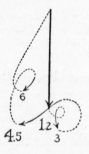

The selection following should be studied with reference to the possibilities of this irregular form in comparison with six beats or two. The *Lullaby* from *Erminie*, once famous, and the well-known *Barcarolle* from Offenbach's *Tales of Hoffmann*, are other examples.

The Last Judgment—*Spohr*

6. By far the greater number of compositions in 6/8 are in a tempo sufficiently rapid to require only two beats to the measure. The two beats in such cases, on *one* and *four*, are *Down-up*, and in typical form, and in their various modifications for music of different styles and *tempi*, are substantially the same as those given for the 2-beat measure (see Chapter Two). As the underlying rhythm of 6/8 is, however, quite different from that of 2/4, the feeling of the conductor is different, and the beat is consequently subtly modified. Though the modification is instinctive and subconscious, as though 6/8 were a mere *style* of 2/4, it may not be amiss to analyze it.

7. When 6/8 is a 2-beat measure, it nevertheless carries an undercurrent of *three to the beat*. In 2/4, if an undercurrent of more rapid notes is suggested, they are characteristically *two* to the beat. Now a longer chain of notes included in one motion, as in the first case, leads to a more sweeping or sustained, or less angular beat. This will be realized if the reader compares his feeling (with respect to the beat) for 2/4, ♫ ♫, with 6/8 ♫♫ ♫♫. The principle may be further

illustrated by comparing the beat one would instinctively give for 2/4 ♩ ♩, with that which he would give for 6/8 ♫♪ ♫♪: for 2/4 ♩ ♩, with 2/4 ♬♬ ♬♬: for 6/8 ♩. ♩. (which is identical with 2/4 ♩ ♩ *unless the undercurrent three-to-the-beat has been established*) with 6/8 ♪.♬♬ ♪.♬♬. *Even when the same tempo is rigidly maintained for both examples in each pair*, the feeling—and therefore the physical response—will be different.

Rapidly moving notes or rhythmic divisions do not have the emphasis or weight at the moment of their entering that attaches to slowly moving notes (or rhythmic divisions). Music in 6/8, even when the measure-form ♩. ♩. is frequent, is seldom long destitute of the clear suggestion of the rapid triple-eighth-note rhythm that distinguishes and forms this measure. The consequence is that in making two beats to a measure in 6/8, a rounded form like this—

will be *more* used, and an angular form like this—

will be *less* used, than in 2/4.

CHAPTER SIX

Phrasing

Through possession of various qualities, tones may be grouped and differentiated into various units of design; and of these music is made.

We have examined the rhythmic groupings termed measures, but a more searching examination of rhythmic facts will be of value to the conductor.

It will be helpful to believe that accents are *born* and not *made*. There is some authority in experimental psychology, it is true, for believing that we instinctively impose what may be termed measure-form upon undifferentiated sounds (such as the ticks of a metronome) and thus group them into twos (rarely threes or fours) beginning with an accent: but this rudimentary rhythmic fact has little significance as we approach the complexities of tonal organization in music—even that organization in music which is purely rhythmic.

In so far as accents are conceived as born out of the nature of tones and not imposed upon an undifferentiated succession by our inner rhythmic mechanism, they are due to the occurrence of a moment of fresher or stronger interest.

A tone may attain superior interest by reason of being, (a) louder; (b) longer; (c) higher or lower; (d) of different quality; (e) the initial note of a pattern. This is equivalent to saying that interest may depend upon (a) Power; (b) Length; (c) Pitch; (d) Quality, or (e) Pattern—or any or all of these.

To illustrate:

(a) Power: Imagine a tone at some one pitch played six

times, in beat lengths, by a violin, as ♩♩♩♩♩♩. By imposing emphasis at various points the series could be organized as 3 × 2 (i.e., ♩♩♩♩♩♩); as 2 × 3 (i.e., ♩♩♩♩♩♩); as 1 × 6 (i.e., ♩♩♩♩♩♩).

(b) **Length**: Lengthening a tone in the series will give it superior interest or accent. E.g., ♩♩♩ ♩♩, immediately causes us to reckon the point of advent of the ♩ as a *point of new departure*, equivalent to accent, or the *beginning of a measure*; and to expect and desire the addition of another half-note to the series, to balance the form created by the first.

(c) **Pitch**: Organization could be created by varying the pitches of the six sounds. Thus, , gives the same impression of 3 × 2 that was created by ♩♩♩♩♩♩;

gives the impression of 2 × 3; while

(see piano accompaniment to C. Bohm's *Still as the Night*), gives the impression of 1 × 6.

(d) **Quality**: If instead of the violin playing the six sounds it were to play only two, and then a clarinet were to play the next two and a trumpet the last two, the impression of 3 × 2 would again be created. If, instead, the violin played three of the notes and a trumpet then played the next three, the impression of 2 × 3 would be created.

(e) **Pattern**: If the tones were given this organization, , it would be difficult to conceive them as other than 3 × 2; if this, , it would be difficult to conceive them as other than 2 × 3. Through memory we recognize the recurrence of a tone-pattern; and the initial moment of this pattern becomes a moment of interest for us.

The list of factors that create interest is probably not complete. Change of harmony (although this might reasonably be included under change of pitch) may deserve special mention. Note its efficacy for rhythmic organization in connection with the following:

Dissonance, as in dissonant chords, organ-points, suspensions, anticipations, impart a sharp tang to moments that might otherwise lack intensity, and are consequently likely to require, or elicit, at the moment of their entrance, a well-defined beat. Highly chromatic harmonies and abrupt and wide changes of key are similarly points of sharp definition.

Ascent in pitch is usually associated with accession in intensity, and descent with diminution in intensity.

All the factors of interest named are present at once, in some degree or other, in any piece of music. There, by their union, they may impart enormous energy to a point; by their dispersal among various voices or instrumental parts give rise to great richness and complexity of structure; by their lack of coordination or irregularities of entry create that competition and clash of accents (interest) which we know as Syncopation. A word of explanation regarding this latter is necessary.

The measure-accent, or metrical accent, (by which, for instance, is meant the *One* and the *three* in a *One*-two-*three*-four), when once established tends to persist in our feeling. If other factors of interest or accent, such as greater length, change of pitch, change of quality, beginning of a pattern, etc., *coincide* with the metrical accent, as they ordinarily do, smoothness and regularity of rhythm obtain. If, on the other hand, the other factors of interest do *not* coincide in time of entry with the established and expected metrical accent, conflict of interests results. For instance, Keller's *American Hymn* begins with these two measures:

Speed our Re - pub-lic

The long note at the beginning coincides with the metrical accent, and the rhythm there is regular: but in the second measure the long note strikes upon the weak 2nd beat, thus imparting strength to it, while at the same time the expected metrical accent on the 3rd beat is engulfed. See also Chapter Two, Par. 4 (b): Mozart's *Entführung aus dem Serail.*

The type of syncopation caused by irregularly placed lengths is the one most discussed, but it is not the only type. That irregularly placed changes of pitch and pattern may be equally efficacious is shown by the following disposition of bars in two illustrations used earlier in this chapter:

The effect of the first two measures is One-two, *three*-one, *two*-three; of the last three measures is One-two-one, *two*-one-two. Irregular placing of any other factor of interest would have had the same effect.

In its broadest sense, phrasing consists in the delicate weighing, balancing, and coordinating into artistic unity the many interests of the various tones and parts of a composition. Only the most sensitive discrimination and the most refined taste can succeed in so responsible and complex an enterprise.

In a very narrow and faulty sense, phrasing is sometimes understood to apply only to the differentiation and separation of successive musical phrases. To indicate such separation with the baton requires a technical action that, though slight, is so important that a separate chapter is reserved for its discussion.

CHAPTER SEVEN

The Phrasing-Beat

The PHRASING-BEAT indicates the termination of a phrase. It consequently has conclusive rather than buoyant character. The effect is gained by a slight dip of the baton, moved from the wrist, approximately in this figure:

This dip is almost invariably coincident with one of the regular metrical beats, and therefore constitutes a mere modification of such beat: and this modification consists principally, if not solely, in making the dip strike below the level that would be struck by the regular, non-phrasing beat.

The effect may be illustrated (perhaps exaggerated as to depth of the phrasing beat) by diagramming the beats appropriate to the first six measures of *America*.

It should be observed that the beat chosen for the first five measures is fairly vigorous and well defined, as for a somewhat large choral group. In the sixth measure, however, the 2nd beat is a sustaining beat, with a somewhat wide lateral swing

44

following the light but clearly defined stroke: and *then ensues the definitive phrasing-beat, with its lowering of the baton.* Observe, too, however, that this phrasing-beat *is immediately followed by a quick rebounding motion upward,* in preparation for the attack on the next phrase: whereas, *were it the final beat of the song,* instead of an early phrase, *it would remain down, relaxing and falling to rest after the stroke marked with a 3.*

In this illustration the phrasing-beat shortened the dotted half-note by one beat—*or appeared to do so.* In other words, it would seem that a quarter-rest was substituted for the dot—the 3rd beat of the 6th measure. This shortening may be lessened, however, as much as desired, by *the manner of making the 2nd beat* of the measure. If this is but lightly struck, is somewhat delayed, and is followed by a slow and still wider floating motion to the right than that shown in the graph, the phrasing-beat will not, or need not, be made until prolongation of the final note (of the phrase or song) has been sufficient. For instance, the last measure of the whole song could be:

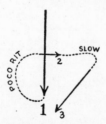

The same effect, in lesser degree, could be used, and is likely to be used, at the end of the first phrase, or any phrase. In fact, *whenever* the phrasing-beat would subtract from the literal or desirable length of the concluding tone of the phrase, this compensating, sustaining, type of beat is likely to be used.

The *phrasing-beat*, as we observed at the end of the 6th measure of *America, by rebounding high, prepares for the attack on the next phrase.* This sort of movement is needed *whenever the end of one phrase and the beginning of the next are on consecutive beats:* i.e., are not separated by rests. The high, signaling movement is made all the more effective by coming after the low, definitive phrasing-beat that terminated the preceding sentence: and since it issues from, or seems an extension of, that definitive stroke, we may say that the *phrasing-beat* often becomes in fact a *Preliminary Beat, quite as important because of what it prophesies as because of what it completes.*

This force of the phrasing-beat as *preliminary beat* is felt particularly in connection with its use after a preluding chord or formal prelude. If, for instance, a preluding chord alone were to be given for *America,* the conductor would probably raise the baton deliberately, and when ready, perhaps after a motionless moment, give a slight, *high-level* phrasing-beat to the accompanist, or accompanists, as a signal for the chord. The speaking-moment of this chord registers on our auditory system merely as a beginning moment: and it is a curious fact that the chord may be of any duration without giving the impression of the passing of beats or measures. At a moment dependent upon the conductor's discretion, however, *the chord is terminated by a phrasing-beat: and this phrasing-beat (made effective also by the cessation of tone) should become metrical by serving as a Preliminary Beat which, rebounding high and thereby signaling the performers, is immediately followed by the Performers' Beat or Attack-Beat.*

It is of great importance that the Performers' Beat should follow the Preliminary Beat at the exact rate of tempo which is to be adopted for the composition. These two beats, the preliminary and the performing, will *together conclusively establish the tempo in the sense of all performers.* Reliance upon this fact will relieve the conductor from the awkward and wholly unnecessary practice of beating an entire measure to establish a tempo. Just as surely as two points determine the direction of a straight line, so do these two beats, the preliminary and the performing, determine a tempo. The student of conducting may test this in his own feeling, in connection with *America*, by counting the *preliminary* beat as "three" and the *performing* beat as "ONE"—

3

1

at different rates of speed. Whatever interval exists between the two moments will impose an inescapable rate of speed upon the beats that follow.

Of course, in connection with the initial attack in orchestra music, or any music that does not require any preluding chord or formal prelude, the preliminary beat, though *it does not then end a tone,* should be made in precisely the same way, should rebound similarly, and should be followed *in tempo,* by the *attack-beat.* While it starts "out of nothing," it is for that reason all the more necessary as a signal and for solidly establishing the tempo. That it is not used to terminate anything in no way affects its character or its decisive effect.

If the stroke which we have called the phrasing-beat is final, indicating the end of the composition (when it is often called the Release or Cut-Off), there is no rebound or recovery whatever: the beat *strikes down and stays there*. If it terminates a preluding phrase or other prelude, or is a sheer preliminary beat coming out of silence, *and is succeeded on the next beat by an attack* (initial or on a new phrase) it then *rebounds high and becomes a signal-beat for the attack*.

One characteristic of the movement remains to be emphasized. The specific phrasing-beat itself is, as we have seen, always the same. The *motion which succeeds* that short, low-descending wrist-stroke is the one that varies and gives the whole gesture the quality either of a *cut-off* or of a *signal*. If phrases are separated by rests (meaning rests that apply to all parts and so create complete silence) the phrasing-beat that precedes the rests is followed *neither by an immediate attack, or by a new section, nor yet by the conclusion of all the musical process*. The baton should therefore not rebound so high as to prompt a premature attack from careless performers, or remain so motionless as to let their perception of rhythmic progress die. As between these two extremes, it should rise to a middle position and simply "mark time" by clear but unassertive beats, *until the last rest-beat is reached*. As that beat precedes an attack, it alone should become a preliminary beat: i.e., a phrasing-beat, *followed by the quick, high rebound that signals the performers*.

This last type of gesture connected with the phrasing-beat may be better realized if diagrammed in connection with music. We again use *America*, as a piece now familiar in this connection, although this time we must mutilate it by rests. By a convenient fiction we may assume that during these rests the music is carried on antiphonally by a choir "off-stage."

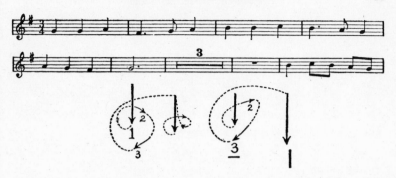

The sensitive modifications of all beats to accord with the musical situations with which they are associated are infinite. One special application (rather than modification) of the phrasing-beat occurs in connection with phrases that begin on a half or third or fourth of a beat. In such cases the attack comes *after* the phrasing-beat—or let us term it now the *Preliminary Beat*—but before the strong, whole, beat which the Preliminary Beat forecasts: and our problem now is to discover what modification of the high rebound (from the preliminary beat) brings the performers in *in advance of the first whole attack-beat.*

We will take for our illustration some measures from

OVERTURE: DIE ZAUBERHARFE, *Schubert*

In the 4th measure of the illustration the 2nd beat is, for flute and first violins, a preliminary or signal beat, to be followed promptly by entrance of flute and first violins on the melody. If the two beats for this 4th measure were made thus—

the entering instruments would *not* be prompted to quick entry. If, instead, they were made thus—

or, in more exaggerated fashion, thus—

quick entry would be stimulated. The difference is not only that the preliminary beat, in the last two figures, *is made at a higher level,* but that *the upward rebound in them is even more elastic and alert than usual*—a factor that the lines can not reveal. The first figure, on the other hand, is so long in the rebound movement that no attack short of the next measure would be elicited. It would be appropriate only if the whole latter part of the 4th measure were rests.

It may be observed, in conclusion, that if the tempo were *very slow* the 2nd beat (of the 4th measure) might be divided thus—

in which case the low phrasing-stroke would not prevent prompt attack on the half-beat. This movement in quick tempo would, however, be futile, because *response can only follow, and can never be simultaneous with movement.* Recognition of this fact will save the conductor from making nervous, rapid gestures that give the *rhythm of the notes instead of the beats.* Such motions only confuse the performers and disturb their rhythmic security. It is quite useless as well as wrong thus to beat the rhythm of notes, *unless the notes so beaten are very slow.*

CHAPTER EIGHT

Other Properties of Beats

Direction is the most fundamental property of the conductor's beat, as it is the most salient. Now that it has been discussed in as strict isolation as was possible, considering that *all* the properties of beats are interdependent, we run no great risk of confusion if, in treating the remaining properties, artificial barriers between them are broken down.

The properties of beats, as we propose to treat them, placed in the order that is most practical for discussion even if it is not the order of their importance, is as follows: 1, (Direction, completed); 2, Extent; 3, Weight; 4, Tension; 5, Elevation; 6, Velocity; 7, Articulation; 8, Advancement.

Length

Extent or length of beat, considered alone and without the addition of other properties, appears to bear a direct relation to the degree of earnestness or vigor of feeling, and *the freedom of release* of that feeling. In this it does not differ from other physical movements; for any movements are slight or restrained in moments of tenderness, delicacy, dreaminess, or doubt, and are free and sweeping when under the impulse of confident power.

Long, sweeping beats would therefore be correlated with moods of confidence, expansiveness, fearlessness, a sense of security. A normal correlative also would be *strength and fullness of tone*. Incidentally, the conductor whose directing elicits a heavy tone and lack of delicacy and refinement of nuance

52

should immediately scrutinize this particular feature of his beat. His beats are probably too large.

Slight or short beats are, it is equally clear, connected with moods that are light, playful, coquettish; subdued, mysterious, breath-taking; dreamy, weary, dull, dispirited. The dynamic correlative is, of course, a small, thin, light tone.

But the number of moods voiced by music, with its subtle possibilities, is infinite, and could not be reflected in the conductor's gestures were the various properties of beats not susceptible of being combined in all varieties of degrees and kinds. Length of beat may have the qualities affirmed above when it is divorced from all other properties, but it assists in portraying many different states of feeling when combined with the remaining properties that are to be described.

Weight

A stroke may be made entirely from the wrist; it may be made by the forearm with more or less cooperation from the wrist; it may be made from the shoulder with more or less cooperation of both forearm and wrist. Indeed, in extreme cases conductors have been observed to move the whole trunk with the beat; but the practice is not recommended to the student.

It is obvious that the above series of movements represents a gradual increase in *weight* of beat, in terms of the sheer physiological mass employed.

Great weight of beat is correlated with qualities of ruggedness, determination, heroic grandeur, profound but almost inarticulate passion, abysmal depths of feeling, colossal tragedy. It is not necessarily correlated with loudness of tone. Thus *Ase's Death* in Grieg's *Peer Gynt* music would look (and feel to the conductor) foolish were it beaten with a wrist-stroke only, even in the *piano* passages. The mood is too deep. Even though the stroke be short (which would ensure small tone) more than the hand from the wrist must be employed. *Morning Mood* or *Anitra's Dance* from the same suite would, on the other hand, be leaden and coarse were a weighty beat employed, however slight its length.

Characteristic examples of music needing considerable weight of beat are much of the Prelude to *Die Meistersinger;* the *Liebestod* from *Tristan;* the beginning of the last movement of Beethoven's *Fifth Symphony;* the reiterated accented notes in the *Intermezzo* from *Cavalleria Rusticana;* the passionate outbursts in the development section of the first movement of Schubert's *Unfinished Symphony,* etc. All heavy, massive accents, indeed, need—and induce, to the sensitive musician—this weighty beat.

Tension

Weight is likely to include the quality of *tension.* Especially in passages that portray inarticulate emotion or writhings of spirit together with small tone, for instance, as in *Ase's Death,* this quality finds play. It is accompanied, quite subconsciously, by tension of many of the muscles of the conductor's arm and hand: and this tension influences the character of the movement and brings, again quite subconsciously, a corresponding change in response from the performers. It is all as instinctive as our awareness of the mood of an animal crouching for a spring—and quite as forceful. Similar communication takes place in connection with all movements of the conductor. It is not telepathy, it is subconscious recognition of the outward signs of feeling, similar to that which makes us respond sensitively to the most delicately differentiated temperaments of the many individuals we meet.

Weight, together with *tension* in some degree or other, is also closely associated with *length;* for while much weight can exist without great length, great length is almost inseparable from considerable weight. The reason is that lengthening the beat necessitates use of first the forearm and, beyond that, the upper arm. Only a comparatively short beat can be made from the wrist alone.

Maximum degrees of *length*, *weight* and *tension* combined, should be reserved for the most overpowering moments. A proper occasion would be the moments of greatest emotional climax in the *Liebestod* from Wagner's *Tristan und Isolde*. Conductors who "throw themselves away" with wide and heavy movements on any lesser occasion disclose lamentable weakness. They reveal either the lack of a sense of artistic proportion, or grossness (in that they can endure and participate in creating generally coarse effects), or fear that they can not control and inspirit the performers with less violent tactics. This latter idea in particular is an illusion. Once a quiet, sensitive, musical atmosphere is created by the conductor's own absorption in the fine qualities of his music, small and sensitive movements have all the command that large movements have when a noisier atmosphere is allowed to gain control.

The combination of *length*, *weight* and *tension* in various degrees and proportions gives many other qualities. A *short* beat combined with much *weight*, especially if in addition there is *tension*, is likely to signify feeling that is tense, repressed inarticulate. Much of the Prelude to Wagner's *Tristan* has this quality. Only recently I heard this Prelude quite spoiled, for me, by a conductor of rare qualities and international fame. It was vapid: the turnings of restless volcanic forces that later burst forth to wreck a spiritual world could not be felt under its soft surface. As my sense of disappointment grew I began to ask what externals of conducting and performance gave rise to the unfortunate quality of effect. I found then that the conductor was giving a beat that was beautiful in its niceties of length and phrasing, and adequate in loud passages in weight as well as in length, but that nowhere had sufficient *tension*. The beat moved with the relaxed grace of a satisfied panther. The violins were sympathetically drawing a quite idyllic but far from intense tone from their instruments by bowing far from the bridge, with comparatively long and light strokes. Nowhere was there hint of tragedy. Why the conductor, who is ordinarily completely responsive, stepped out of his rôle as participant in the drama for those few precious moments I can not imagine.

A *long* beat combined with *weight* but lacking *tension* gives an impression (due to the length) of freedom, and one (due to the weight) of determination. Vigorous purpose, unhindered energy, are expressed (and induced) by such a beat. The glowing Prelude to the Third Act of *Lohengrin*, the *Ride of the Valkyrie*, or the Prelude to *Carmen* might well be thus expressed.

Length in greater proportion than *weight* is in accord with joy, abandon, ecstasy, rather than earnest purpose. As weight is added the corresponding mood appears to be more one of determination, irresistible will. The opening measures of Beethoven's *Fifth Symphony*, or the characteristic announcements of the *Siegfried* motive may well exemplify this quality. Add *tension* and the suggestion is that of great force that is struggling, that may be doomed to defeat. The *Liebestod* from *Tristan* can not be surpassed as a familiar example of this latter quality.

Elevation

This property of beats is not so important as some that follow, but is introduced here because closely allied with the expressional qualities that have been discussed in connection with *length, weight* and *tension.*

The property was mentioned in Chapter Seven, The Phrasing-Beat. There it was pointed out that depressing or elevating the beat led, respectively, to the feeling of cessation, finality, or to a feeling of expectation.

The more the beat, within resonable limits, is elevated, the more does it accord with a feeling of elevation. Lightness, buoyancy, delicacy; the fairy-like, the celestial, the seraphic; jubilation, happiness, aspiration, joy, exaltation, apotheosis; all these require elevation of beat. As a few appropriate musical examples we may mention the *Scherzo* from Mendelssohn's *Midsummer Night's Dream; Anitra's Dance* from Grieg's *Peer Gynt;* the *Dance of the Sylphs* from Berlioz's *Damnation of Faust; Unfold Ye Portals Everlasting,* from Gounod's *Redemption;* portions of the latter part of Strauss' *Death and Transfiguration.* The list could, of course, be multiplied indefinitely.

But the compositions mentioned, though they all possess some of the qualities named above as in accord with an elevated beat, are certainly very far from being alike. Their different qualities are therefore expressed by *combining other properties, in various proportions, with elevation.*

Length and *weight* qualify and individualize greatly the general mood of buoyancy reflected by an elevated beat. A long or a heavy beat, or still more a long *and* heavy beat, is inconceivable in connection with *Anitra's Dance* or the Mendelssohn *Scherzo.* In *Unfold Ye Portals,* however, both these properties could and should be added. To make a beat appropriate to the latter the elbow will be raised *at the side* almost level with the shoulder, and the forearm, moved or pushed to some extent by the upper arm, which thus adds *weight*, will describe sweeping, vigorous beats, punctuated sharply by decisive strokes from the wrist at the moment of the ictus. A less vigorous and broad state of elevated feeling would be expressed, either by elevating the elbow less, or by elevating it *in front* instead of at the side of the body—thus lessening the action of the upper arm and consequently diminishing the *weight* of the stroke—or by adopting both procedures.

Velocity and Articulation

The two properties, *velocity* and *articulation*, are so closely connected that they can be discussed most profitably together.

Velocity does not connote tempo. By velocity is meant the rapidity with which the baton describes any single stroke. The movement may be swift and incisive or slow and floating.

In following these analyses of beats it is always advisable to hold some musical example in mind to which the styles of beat described may be applied. Unless this is done the descriptions will lack in meaning.

One characteristic use of a swift beat is in connection with crisp, *staccato* passages. We will take, as our example, *Anitra's Dance, Peer Gynt Suite*, Grieg, already mentioned in connection with *elevation* of beat. If this piece is performed in imagination at the traditional tempo, *while the reader beats time*, it will soon become manifest that the inclination is toward a swiftly performed and detached or "dry" beat. A little experimenting will prove, however, that, *without delaying the tempo a whit*, a more slowly moving and smoothly connected beat is possible—but, of course, only to the complete destruction of the proper style of performance.

But observe that with the beat moving swiftly the strokes are detached, and with it moving slowly, *though in the same tempo*, the beats are connected. The music in the one case would (properly) be *staccato*, in the other would be *legato*. It is this connection of one beat with another that we discuss under the term *articulation*.

The discussion will be clearer if we recall that at the outset beats were said to be *points in time* rather than *duration*. There is, therefore, an interval between beats, as we recognize when the beats are clicked by a metronome. This interval may be employed by *a slow movement of the baton toward the point where* (*or toward the moment when*) the beat is struck: or the baton may be held back until the beat-moment has arrived, and then move *all at once* to its next decisive point.

But observe again that if the movement of the hand is delayed, as described, each beat will be disjoined from its predecessor. The swift movement thus not only *strikes* a beat, but further marks it by *arrest of motion:* and in the interval between *arrest* and *stroke* the hand is still.

The swift movement makes for animation; the detachment makes for *staccato* quality. If the swift detached movement is from the wrist only, and therefore lacks both *length* and *weight*, and (which is of still more importance) if *elevation* is given it, we have a beat appropriate to *Anitra's Dance* or the *Scherzo* from *Midsummer Night's Dream*. Increase of length and weight —and apply this, in imagination, to *Anitra's Dance*—will immediately introduce a feeling of greater power, determination, or even of ruggedness, sinister purpose or malevolence. Especially if the beat is lowered while swift, weighty and detached strokes are continued, is the grim or evil quality likely to be suggested. The moods of, for instance, *In the Hall of the Mountain King*, from *Peer Gynt*, Grieg, are more appropriately reflected by a weightier and lower *staccato* beat, than are the moods of *Anitra's Dance*.

It should be observed that velocity and articulation are characteristically in inverse proportion: that is to say, when the beats are swift they are characteristically disjointed or separate, when they are made slowly they merge into one another. In very *sostenuto* passages the incisive "bite" of the beats frequently disappears almost entirely, and a very slight inflection of the baton, or even a mere arrest or momentary hesitation in its movement makes a soft throb or swelling wave of what, in more decisive rhythms, would be a sharply defined beat. This flowing beat, in which articulation is very close, is appropriate, for instance, in much of the *Intermezzo* from *Cavalleria Rusticana* or for the horn quartet in the following introductory movement:

OVERTURE: DER FREISCHÜTZ, *von Weber*

OVERTURE: DER FREISCHÜTZ, *von Weber* (**continued**)

The movement appropriate to these measures is of very low velocity—is of such nature, indeed, as almost to give the impression that a beat *is* a duration, and *not* a point in time, as we have insisted. The slow, level glide of the movement is punctuated, however, by very slight inflections of the baton at the beat-moments; and these impart the throb of pulsation to what would otherwise be an oily, featureless, flow.

Among infinite blendings and gradations one other type of beat (or music) should, perhaps, be distinguished in connection with *velocity* and *articulation*. Its chief characteristic is low velocity combined with well-marked articulation.

The music which is appropriately reflected by such a beat is likely to possess breadth, gravity, dignity, nobility, and strength, all combined. As an illustration of the style we cite the aria from Handel's forgotten opera *Xerxes*, familiarly known as the Handel *Largo*.

Air from Xerxes, *Handel*

Unquestionably the beats for this strain may not be swiftly struck, for the flowing quality that is clearly predominant would thereby be destroyed. On the other hand, the beats certainly do not merge imperceptibly into one another as a mere sub-surface swelling, as was the case in the *Der Freischütz* excerpt. On the contrary, the stately, punctual, tread of beat-length quarter-notes is an impressive and characteristic feature of the composition.

The beat that would reflect these qualities would, of course, have fair length and weight and some elevation. The combination of low velocity and distinct articulation is attained by imposing upon the slow, broad, solid movement thus established a modified form of the slight, punctuating stroke that was described earlier in Chapter Two. Instead of a slight dip punctuating the general, broadly waving movement, we need now a stroke of much the same quality, but one that starts higher than the wrist. In short, the broad general movement involves the upper arm from the shoulder to a slight extent, the forearm to a greater extent, and the wrist, *plus some contributory motion from the forearm,* for the punctuating stroke.

Advancement

The baton may move in a field close to the body or it may be advanced far in front. When it is drawn in most closely the upper arm is at the side of the body or is even drawn back of it a little, and the forearm is folded back close to the upper arm.

If it plays farther forward, the advancement is obtained first by unbending the arm at the elbow, next by moving the upper arm forward from the shoulder. The range is thus from a position that may be suggested by bringing the hands back against the lapels of one's coat, to one that is suggested by extending the arms straight out from one's shoulders.

The effect upon the performers of regression in position is one of reserve, caution or repression. Animation, free and unhesitant release of feeling and action are, comparatively, indicated by the advanced baton. There is command, the imperative quality, in either: but the withdrawn baton counsels care, cautious restraint, and the advanced baton counsels free and prompt action, unhesitating release. If command is conceived as always positive, if it is to do right instead of to be careful to do nothing overmuch or wrong, then there is more command in the advanced beat.

Precautionary command may be applied to almost any effect. The baton is almost always drawn back, for instance, for *pianissimo*, whispering or "dying-away" effects, thus indicating restraint or repression in the amount of tone. Coupled with elevation and very short, light beats, regression might mean "as daintily as possible." Used in a beat made at a lower level and with considerable weight (but not great length) as in *Asa's Death*, it might rather reflect restraint in free movement, a brooding and tense quality. Or combined with a more freely moving beat, it might betoken the rapt dream, vision, the spellbound moment, as opposed to bright and wide-awake action.

The qualities reflected by the advanced position of the arm and baton are already suggested, by implication, as opposites of effects consonant with the withdrawn baton. Besides qualities of musical effect, however, advancement of the baton is an effective means for producing response, action, from all or from particular groups or individuals among the performers. To advance the baton "under the nose" of a clarinet or trombone player whose duty it is at the moment to contribute an important musical statement to the whole discourse is to stimulate him immediately to complete attention and whole-souled effort. Conductors are constantly turning and advancing the baton thus toward players or singers whose part, at the moment, bears the weight of greatest interest. Often, indeed, one will see the conductor reinforce even the insistence of this appeal by instinctively inclining his whole body toward the performers with whom he wishes to establish the greatest *rapport*, and from whom he wishes the greatest warmth of utterance.

Apart from the Baton

Bodily pose and facial expression certainly contribute somewhat to the conductor's indications of his musical intentions, but just as certainly they are not subject to technical treatment and so need not be discussed. Besides, no one should ever become self-conscious with respect to them, unless to repress them! No weakness in conducting, in fact, equals that which is represented by a conductor with little or no technique who assumes a pose and a facial expression presumably appropriate to the nature of the music, and then endeavors to make such general emotional intention discharge his conductorial job. On the other hand, of course, one should not rigidly suppress all facial and bodily expression, and if one is really musical he can not do so. No truly musical person could stand and look the same while conducting the *Meistersinger Prelude*, for instance, as while conducting the first movement of Tschaikowsky's *Sixth*

Symphony. Intention, however, would be absent in both cases. The good conductor would simply live from moment to moment in the music, and apart from his technique of control would make no effort to express emotional intentions. In truth, he would be too busy and too engrossed musically to become histrionic. If subconsciously he revealed the deep and broad emotional states that underlay the music, that revelation would have the value of an unsought but rich by-product, to be accepted so long as it did not, through exaggeration, interfere with the real conductorial task.

Keeping Long Tones Alive

One additional application of such expressional baton-technique as we have discussed is perhaps sufficiently important to deserve mention. It concerns long tones, either upheld by rhythmical pulsations or existing as somewhat rhythmless extensions of tone, as in the case of notes marked by a Pause or Hold. Seldom, if ever, should the life be permitted to die out of such tones by reason of the conductor adopting a purely mechanical beat or ceasing to beat altogether. No tone, in fact, should be permitted to stretch out like a factory whistle, without modification, nuance or purpose, beyond the length of a slow beat or two. It should increase, diminish, grow more or less intense, or be palpitant with life and intention in some way. For illustration consider the first measures sung by the chorus in Brahms' *German Requiem,* as presented in the excerpt following.

GERMAN REQUIEM, *Brahms*

It is inconceivable that the first or the second tone here should be sung throughout with precisely the quality and power it had on the attack. But what delicate modifications should invest the tones with life and how should these be indicated by the conductor? Possibly *elevation* (rise of level) of beat is the only modifying factor. If in the first measure the 2nd beat were at a slightly lower level than the 3rd, the corresponding almost imperceptible swell would be appropriate. In the next measure, contrastingly, the level of beat might well rise continuously, producing a slight—a *very* slight—increase in power throughout. But the quarter-note, "they," in the third measure would then need to be guarded against vigor and abruptness, by means of a slow, sinking beat (i.e., one of low Velocity) that would elicit a quiet and sustained tone that would let the phrase down tenderly.

The "factory-whistle" effect is particularly objectionable in long tones taken *forte.* Choruses are especially susceptible to this fault, and the yelling effect produced by many a chorus is due less to volume than to the unbearable monotony of a loud tone that persists pitilessly. There seems to be no sentient being back of such a tone; it is unhuman. Climacteric *fortissimo* cadence-chords, at the close of long compositions, often invite this unpleasant treatment. The wise conductor will either reserve the greatest volume of tone for the very last part of the last beat, will make *marcato* effects take the place of sustained loudness, or will produce other variations, dependent upon the character of the music, that will avoid the deadly danger of sheer vociferousness. *But none of these fluctuations can be produced if the conductor stops beating time.* It is therefore a good rule, even through a note with a Hold over it, *to continue beating time, although at a retarded tempo and with a slight wrist-stroke only to punctuate the beat, which may be as wide, flowing, high and tense as the strength of tone and character of mood demand.* (See earlier in this chapter the discussion of "punctuated" beat illustrated by the introduction to Weber's *Overture to Der Freischütz* and by Handel's *Largo*.) The movement between beats, in such cases, keeps the music alive with *feeling* of the appropriate kind; and the marking of the beat-moments, even though these are irregular, is not without importance, for such marking keeps the music from dying *rhythmically*.

CHAPTER NINE

Divided Beats

The fundamentals of conducting are discussed in the foregoing chapters and the student who has mastered them will
have little difficulty in projecting his technique into the further
musical ranges we shall enter. Not that this book is intended
to be thoroughly comprehensive. Indeed, since music is infinite
in its variety, a treatise that would endeavor to include every
rhythmic and expressional variety of music that might be en-
countered would be under the necessity of examining every
piece of music in existence in considerable detail—a manifest
impossibility. The conductor must realize from the first that
no two pieces, or no two measures of the same composition,
even, have exactly the same contour, weight, intention and atmosphere, and that if he makes them alike the result will be
comparatively stupid mechanicalism. Nevertheless, at the risk
of unduly extending what is intended to be merely a helpful
handbook, discussion of some additional problems appears
necessary.

Divided Beats

A negative word of caution is so important here that it
should perhaps precede any positive instruction. It is this: *Do
not beat notes* (except in rare cases to be discussed later) *but
beat beats.*

There are good reasons for the foregoing prohibition. First,
the rhythm created by the speaking-moments of the tones owes
a great deal of its interest and charm *to the way in which it is
laid on the beat-rhythm or the measure-rhythm.* Thus ♩ ♩♩ ♩,

as a note-rhythm is dull, but laid on an established 3-beat measure-rhythm becomes abrupt and vigorous. This is a crude illustration of a fact that applies to all music except the greater number of *cadenzas* and *recitatives*. Since the notes themselves establish note-rhythm by their moments of speaking, the conductor who makes motions coincidently adds nothing to that rhythm while he does sacrifice the values that arise from the particular lay-out of the note-rhythm upon the ground-pattern of beat- and measure-rhythms.

The conductor afflicted with the bad habit of beating note-rhythms thinks that he thereby obtains greater clearness and security of attack. On the contrary, once the periodic beat-rhythm is abandoned, the performers have no means of estimating a moment of attack until the moment is upon them. Attack would then need to be simultaneous with the movement of the baton, and as this is impossible, precision, unanimity and artistic quality are all lost. Attacks, in short, must be forecast, must not be adventitious but must be moments in some sort of *measured* flow. To this end the conductor must prefigure each moment as certainly as the initial attack is prefigured by a Preliminary Beat: and only through indicating some rate of beat-motion, however flexibly this is modified, can he attain such result.

However, the term Divided Beats, as understood in conducting, does not imply breaking beats into *note-values*, but rather dividing inordinately long beats into shorter ones. Regularity of beat-rhythm is not thereby lost, but rapid beats are substituted for slow ones. Nevertheless the topics are connected, because *very* rapid beats, even if regular, agitate and destroy the measured flow and defeat the responses of the performers almost as greatly as do note-rhythm beats. In short, perception of a beat and response to it can not occur at once: and if this were universally recognized we should not have the spectacle occasionally observed, of a conductor beating twice as hard as he should in an effort to secure rhythmic unanimity among his performers, and obtaining results much poorer than those that he would get were he to make only half as many beats. Indeed, a paragraph might well be inserted here counselling the *merging* rather than the *division* of beats. Often a passage in 4-beat measure will become so rapid that it is better indicated and controlled by making, for a time, two beats only to the measure. Musical feeling and experience are the only guides the conductor has in deciding such matters.

But beats that are too slow, that succeed one another at too long intervals, create vacuities between beats, during which the sense of rhythmic periodicity and of emotional life dies out, and the conductor is without power, motion having been exhausted, to give any indication of the musical intentions and effects that should be steadily unfolded.

The lower limit of effective rate, below which beats should be divided, thus becomes the first practical question for the conductor. It might be unmistakably stated in metronomic terms if the nature of the music—its note-rate, the length and character of its phrases and motives—were not so varied and so influential. It may be said, in general, that when the tones are of beat-length or greater, very slow beats are effective; but when the *tonal* movement is more rapid, with two to four or more tones to the beat, the tonal patterns will be in terms of fractions of beats and will accordingly require divided beats for their delineation. For illustration compare the two excerpts following:

Symphony No. 6, *Tschaikowsky*

Air from Suite in D Major, *Bach-Wilhelmj*

Although in connection with the first illustration the sensitive dynamic markings must be indicated by noticeable degrees of *elevation* and *extent* of beat, the beats, however slow, do come upon the appropriate moments in the music and there is no difficulty, in the intervals between them, in controlling the dynamic expression. The appropriateness of the long beat in the first example will be still more forcefully recognized if the student will imagine beating eight beats to the measure instead. The result is so absurd as to need no discussion. The only points in the Tschaikowsky excerpt at which division of beat might be in the least appropriate are those at which the bassoon has two eighth-notes to the beat. Here a mere interruption of motion in the middle of the up-beat—a stoppage and resumption of motion—might enable the conductor to indicate more accurately to the performer the required increase in power. On the other hand, adoption of a rate of only four beats to the measure for the Bach piece would ruin it. Such a rate might be conceivable for the first measure if the pattern sketched by the 'cello and bass were omitted from consideration; but the suggestion is made only to stimulate thought, for of course such omission is musically inconceivable. In the second measure of the same selection not only the bass parts, but also the solo part obviously require, for elucidation and control, eight beats—or rather four beats divided—to the measure.

Substitution of Measure-Forms

Before describing the forms taken by divided beats, a distinction should be made between *dividing beats* and *substituting other forms of measure*. The latter practice is likely to occur in connection with 2/4 measures. Sometimes a composition designated as 2/4 not only requires four strokes in a measure but is built of forms that imply a 4-beat, rather than a divided 2-beat, conception. In such cases there is no fault in adopting a 4/8 beat, since in reality the music is organized in a 4/-measure. On the other hand, if a 2-beat basis is implied, by the predominance of long notes or by delicate factors of phrase-structure, a 4-beat form of movement would be incorrect, and the divided down-beat and divided up-beat should be substituted. Often there are border-line cases that are difficult of distinction, and frequently, too, different sections of a long composition will require different treatment. Moreover, the superior grace, comfort and authority of the 4-beat movement, as compared with the divided 2-beat, sometimes impels its adoption when the music itself might well cast doubt upon such a choice. On the whole, however, music presents a great number of clearly defined cases of both types, and the inexperienced conductor should at least know the possible alternatives and the bases of choice. As profitable examples for study we suggest: Beethoven, *Third Symphony* (*Eroica*), second movement (*Marcia funebre, Adagio assai*); Haydn, *Surprise Symphony*, second movement (*Andante*); Mozart, *Symphony in E-flat Major*, second movement (*Andante*). Many small and comparatively unimportant pieces will provide further examples, equally helpful to the student for technical purposes if not of equal musical worth. The older classicists, however, Bach, Handel, Haydn, and Mozart, provide more numerous examples of the divided beat, for it was a frequent practice with them to use C, and sometimes 2/4, as measure-signatures for music which could only be held together by beating an eighth-note rhythm. Handel's *Messiah* provides a strikingly large number of instances, among which are the solos *Comfort Ye* and *He Was Despised*, and the chorus, *Surely He Hath Borne Our Griefs*. As all of these have the value of eight eighth-notes to the measure, there is no question, in connection with them, of *substituting another form of measure*, because there is no 8-beat measure-form for the baton. Such an alternative, indeed, can arise only in connection with a 2-beat versus a 4-beat measure: for a 3/ can not become a 6/ when the number of impulses per measure is doubled, because the 6/ indicates *two groups of three* and the divided 3/ indicates *three groups of two*; a 4/ has no alternative 8/; and a divided 6/ can not become a 12/, because a 6/ divided is rhythmically 6 × 2, while a 12/ is 4 × 3.

It is of the utmost importance that the student should not think that a whole-beat rate or a half-beat rate, once adopted for a composition, must be adhered to throughout. It is true that there are many compositions in which the metronomic marking, as in the citations above, is given in terms of half-beat units, and usually in such cases the indicated form and rate of beat is consistently maintained. Even in these, however, an *accelerando* might require a *merging of half-beats into whole beats;* and subdivisions of even the half-beat, in case of *ritardandos*, are not unknown. On the other hand, a much greater number of compositions bear metronomic markings (or have a known rate) expressed in terms of whole-beat units, and in this imposing group the given rate and form of beat is certainly not to be understood as requiring inflexible adherence throughout. In practice, indeed, the conductor will probably employ the divided beat more frequently as a transient deviation from such established whole-beat forms than as a long continued beat adopted as the prescribed and ruling form. Any *ritardando* may, indeed, retard whole beats to dangerous limits and therefore urgently call for a division of beats; and it must not be forgotten that, conversely, any acceleration may crowd beats to a point of indistinguishable flight, and therefore make the merging of beats necessary. The brief excerpt from *Cavalleria Rusticana,* quoted later in this chapter, illustrates the point; for the entire *Intermezzo* from which the measures are taken is certainly not beaten with the divided beat, although at the point cited, and at several other points, that beat must be employed.

Forms of Movement

The form of movement adopted for the divided beat may be succinctly stated. In general, the movement that delineates a beat is succeeded by another and subordinate movement in the same direction. Thus, a divided 2/ is *Down*, down, *Up*, up; a divided 3/ is *Down*, down, *Right*, right, *Up*, up; a divided 4/

is *Down*, down, *Left*, left, *Right*, right, *Up*, up; and a divided
6/ would similarly add to each of the six movements diagrammed earlier a second, subordinate movement in the same
direction. A divided 6/ is, however, very rare, because 6/8 ordinarily requires contraction rather than expansion, and the extent of a measure of 6/4 or 6/2 is already so great that were
it lengthened to include twelve "throbs" at slow *tempo* it would
exceed our psychological power of measure-perception. This
sort of limitation of our power of rhythm-perception accounts
for the fact that we do not have 9/4, 12/4, or 9/2, 12/2 measures. The ONE in so long a series of deliberate beats would be
so delayed in returning that when it did return its relation to
the last preceding ONE would be lost, and we should have no
feeling of a recurring cycle.

Limiting our diagrams, then, to the divided beat in 2/, 3/
and 4/ measures, we may delineate the movements as follows:

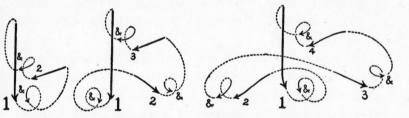

As with all such figures, it is difficult to make the lines tell
the truth; and moreover, any or all of the modifications discussed in connection with whole beats may be needed in connection with these half-beats according to the quality or style
of the music delineated. It seems unnecessary to attempt diagrams of these many modifications of divided beats, after what
has been said in connection with whole beats, but some special
variations may be summarized in words.

(a) In the diagrams the second half of each beat is *subordinated* to the first half of each beat, the indication being that the second half is weaker and is accordingly expressed by a shorter stroke than the first half. This would be true of normal rhythms, but, as we have seen earlier, many passages in music depart from the ordinary ratios of strength and interest. For instance, study such a passage as this:

CAVALLERIA RUSTICANA, *Mascagni*

The last half of the 2nd beat and both halves of the 3rd beat are all approximately equal and the movement for one of the three eighth-notes should be as extensive and decisive as for the others.

(b) The Articulation of the second half of a beat with the first half is not always so elaborate as that indicated in the diagrams. If the tempo is rapid or (and) the music cool and unemotional, the 2nd half-beat, instead of being a fairly elaborate stroke that starts from a separate impulse, may be a mere *continuation* of the impulse that made the 1st half-beat, and be divided from that first half only by a momentary arrest of motion. *Down*, down, for example, would then be literally descriptive of the movement; and it might be further described by saying that it has the character of *one down-beat divided*, while the more florid divided-beat movement graphically outlined has the character of *two down-beats* in succession. Of course, between an extremely "dry" 2nd half-beat and the one floridly executed, there are many delicate gradations of emphasis.

An important use of the transient divided beat, the frequent need of which was mentioned on p. 74, is the delineation of phrase-joints in the case of phrases that begin on the last half of a beat. Now that the form of divided-beat movements has been explained, this remaining application may be discussed. The measures following those recently quoted from *Cavalleria Rusticana* will serve us well here for illustration:

CAVALLERIA RUSTICANA, *Mascagni*

Ignoring the first three notes of the illustration, and beginning with the first full measure, the conductor will feel that that measure requires a whole (undivided) Down-beat, and a 2nd, or right-beat, that begins as *continuation of tone* and so without any intimation of coming division. But the moment that tone, a beat and a half long, ends, a joint, a *new departure*, occurs. The last half of the 2nd beat is divided, in short, from the first half of the beat. No conductor with a proper feeling for phrasing and a desire for niceties and precision of response would here wave a flowing and undivided 2nd beat. On the other hand, once the 2nd beat is divided, a whole-beat movement may be resumed, because to cut the 3rd beat of the same measure into halves would break the three eighth-notes of the motive, here properly united, into separate fragments. The movements for the measure would accordingly be

The last half of the up-beat might, it is true, be divided by the slightest arrest of motion, and without a feeling of discontinuity, from the first half, but the need is doubtful. In the ensuing measure, however, the continued retardation bespeaks a different condition, and there the 2nd beat is not only divided by a separately propelled last half-beat, but the 3rd beat is divided by a slight pause, succeeded by a continuation of the gentle, lifting motion that is made largely by elevation of the arm.

In the two matters of proportioning and articulating the 2nd half-beat, that fraction of the rhythm has been considered largely with respect to varying degrees of *difference* from the 1st half-beat which might give it individual character. Usually, however, the student may expect the 2nd half-beat to reflect the same qualities as the 1st half-beat, although generally with a lesser degree of rhythmic force. The distinction may become clearer if we separate (somewhat arbitrarily, it is true) *rhythmic expression* from general *moods*. With respect to rhythmic accentuation and independence the 2nd half-beat may be more or less akin to, or be separate from, the 1st half-beat. A *general musical atmosphere or mood* is likely, however, to pervade long stretches of music uniformly, and in such cases both half-beats reflect that general nature of the music uniformly. Thus a long, flowing beat, or a weighty, determined beat, or a dainty, elevated beat, may be indicated by the music, and will then equally affect all beats and all half-beats throughout a long succession of measures. But during the passage, with respect to fine details of rhythmic emphasis, the 2nd half-beat, as compared with the 1st, may be more or less long, weighty, perhaps tensed, and be more or less connected with, or separated from, the 1st half-beat. At such moments it will probably not lose its general character—say, of *elevation*—but will, of course, reflect the proper rhythmic balances with the utmost nicety.

CHAPTER TEN

Nine, Twelve, Five and Seven Beats, Recitatives and Cadenzas

The comparative uneasiness and discomfort of beating divided beats, to which we alluded earlier, arises from the necessity of making consecutive motions in the same direction, whereas, as was said (Chapter One, Par. 8) our muscles adapt themselves more readily to reversal of direction. The awkwardness is not felt to a great extent when beats are divided in two, but in connection with the three-fold division, which we will next consider, it becomes more pronounced.

Fortunately, measures that require nine beats or twelve beats are rare, because in 9/8 and 12/8 the rate of motion for eighth-notes is usually so rapid that the dotted quarter-note— ♩. — becomes the unit of measurement, with the result that the measures are beaten, respectively, like 3/4 and 4/4. Nevertheless, the necessity for actually beating nine beats and twelve beats arises quite frequently, and the conductor's technique with respect to them should be developed. The topic has been delayed to follow the preceding chapter because the required movements have precisely the same characteristics as divided-beat movements. This will be seen from what follows.

A 9/8 is ordinarily, as was said, beaten as a 3/4; but since each beat embraces a triple rhythm of three eighth-notes, the beats, if divided at all, are divided in *threes*. Similarly the beats in 12/8, ordinarily four in number and beaten like a 4/4, divide, if at all, into *threes*. The form of beat, then, for 9/8 (as nine eighth-notes, not three dotted quarter-notes) is *Down*, down, down, *Right*, right, right, *Up*, up, up: and the form of beat for

12/8 (as *twelve eighth-notes*, not four dotted quarter-notes) is *Down*, down, down, *Left*, left, left, *Right*, right, right, *Up*, up, up.

Delineation of these movements is difficult, but the following will suggest the essentials of the forms:

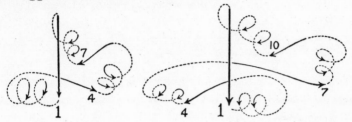

As always, the figures are misleading because the paths of later beats often, in practice, cross the paths of the earlier ones, and delineation of the true paths would appear as an inextricable tangle. The beats are moreover subject to various degrees of downward inflection, corresponding to the emphasis that may be demanded of each. This is especially true of the essential beats—the 1, 4, 7, and, in 12/8, the 10. The secondary and tertiary strokes are not so likely to demand emphasis, since characteristically these measures move lightly and flowingly. An *allargando* or *ritardando* might, however, require detailed emphasis of separate eighth-notes. Needless to say, pervasive moods may modify the forms shown.

Measures of 5/4, 7/4, and other irregular forms are likely to perplex the inexperienced conductor. A measure of 5/4 is likely to consist of 2/4 + 3/4 and in that case is beaten

It may be described as *Down*, up *down*, right, up. Care must be taken not to raise the baton far on the 2nd beat, for the ensuing *down* might then be indistinguishable from the *Down* that begins the measure. The classic example is:

SYMPHONY No. 6, *Tschaikowsky*, Second Movement

The beat is characteristically a "dry" beat, and while dynamics must be indicated there is little need for *striking* any beat with a heavy impulse.

Occasionally a 5/4 is 3/4 + 2/4. An excellent example is from Harvey B. Gaul's cantata, *Tubal Cain*.

The excerpt quoted consists of measures 6 to 9 inclusive of the orchestral prelude. An appropriate form of beat for these measures is

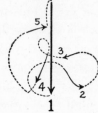

TUBAL CAIN, *H. B. Gaul*

Measures of 7/4 sometimes occur. Their rhythmic construction may be 3/4 + 4/4 or 4/4 + 3/4. As illustrating the first type, no better example can be found than that which follows.

Like the preceding example, it is taken from Harvey Gaul's cantata, *Tubal Cain*, and the quotation embraces measures 15 to 20 inclusive of the instrumental prelude. The whole example, necessitating as it does a constant alternation between two unusual forms of measure, shows the practical technical difficulties that may at any time confront the conductor. Any except the most experienced and routined conductor is likely to be obliged to spend a little time in practicing baton technique and getting the "feel" of the appropriate beat "into his arm" before he conducts easily and musically the music here cited.

TUBAL CAIN. *H. B. Gaul*

A 7/4 with the rhythm of 4/4 + 3/4 characterizes this folk-song:

BRETON FOLK-SONG, *Traditional*

A graph of either type of 7/4 is difficult to construct because the lines cross and because in practice the baton may actually retrace on later beats (sometimes in forward and sometimes in reverse direction) the path pursued by earlier beats. This is true of REPEATED *Downs*, *rights*, etc., and of *down* as related to *up*, and of *right* as related to *left* movements. The difficulty is inescapable; but allowance must be made for it when the two graphs following are studied.

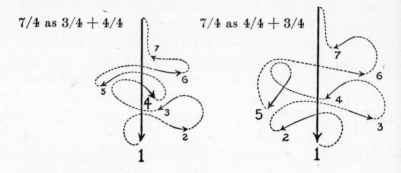

7/4 as 3/4 + 4/4   7/4 as 4/4 + 3/4

The most helpful fact to remember in connection with all forms of 5/4 and 7/4 is that they combine two measure-forms in one, that they always contain two *down*-beats, and that the second *down* must not take its start from as high a point as the first. If the student will remember this he can place the graphs for 2/4 and 3/4 (or 3/4 and 2/4) side by side and merely join them (for 5/4), beating the second of the two *in miniature* until the beat has become fluent. The components of 7/4, 3/4 and 4/4 (or 4/4 and 3/4), may be similarly treated. Remember that the 1st *up*-beat must not rise high if the 2nd *down* is to remain subordinate to the *Down* that begins a measure.

Recitatives

Two points must receive attention in conducting accompaniments for recitatives: the beginning of each measure must be marked by a clearly distinguished down-beat, and the entrance of every chord must be forecast. Further, there is feeling and movement in a recitative (though the movement is irregular) and if the feeling and movement are to be participated in by the conductor and be evident through his means of expression, namely, his baton, this can not be at a standstill but must be in motion. The manner of conducting a recitative that consists of marking the measures and then leaving the baton quiescent till it is called upon to snap forth a chord is therefore ill-advised. It fails alike to keep the players imbued with the impulses and feelings that invest the recitative, and to delineate the details of rhythmic structure. The result is likely to be responses that are devoid of the reigning musical quality and that lack quiet precision.

The best practice is therefore to beat all the beats, but unobtrusively, the beats during which the accompaniment rests being merely outlined in small movements made in front of the body. These beats, though unobtrusive, need not lack in quality. *Elevation, length* (comparatively, within a small scale), *weight, tension* and other qualities may be made evident in them, and will, indeed, unavoidably be present if the conductor truly *accompanies* the soloist throughout, in feeling as well as in rhythmic responses. They will, of course, differ from regular beats in being of varying durations. In fact they will merely drift along with the soloist by means of a slow, "sneaking" motion, until such time as a certain number of notes have been uttered, and will then set up a beat-marker (by means of a very slight wrist-stroke given the baton) as an indication that one section of the measure has been delivered. This will be continued until a punctuating chord is to enter. Just before this chord the beat will spring to life with a quick preliminary or signaling "dip," followed immediately by the characteristic rebound upward; and the chord will then enter as the ensuing motion (beat or half-beat) is delivered. It is important to observe, however, that in such case *the preliminary beat does not precede the attack beat at a regular interval but is merely a flash signal that requires immediate response.* The reason is that there is no regular beat-rhythm to be followed or to be established. The beat—or even several beats—preceding the attack may have gone by with a rushing irregularity that made prediction impossible, and those that follow will be similarly irregular. The best that can be done, therefore, is to chart the irregular beat-sections as they come, and indicate action from the players at such point as far in advance as possible.

The foregoing explanation and suggestions will hold little practical value if merely read once. They should rather be read slowly and repeatedly, while a baton is held in the reader's hand and his eyes fall from time to time on the musical example given below. By applying the recommended form of conducting to the example, in imagination, its practical bearings will become evident and can be tested. Even more than is specifically directed can, indeed, be done; for if the moods of scorn and defiance implicit in the given excerpt are rightly felt and expressed, some specific qualitative property, over and above the mere time-indications, will be added.

ELIJAH, *Mendelssohn*

The Cadenza

The formal, classical cadenza, unlike the recitative, does call for a complete cessation of baton-motion. The conductor need only, by his quiescence, leave his performers in unapprehensive quiet until the moment of their entry approaches, and then, by a quiet lifting of the baton, put them in a state of readiness. This signal to a state of preparedness, which with an orchestra, for instance, would indicate that instruments were to be lifted into playing-position, should not be given too long in advance or be so abrupt as to lead to hasty action that would attract the attention of the audience. Given rightly, the instruments will be put quietly in position for playing a moment or two before they are to be played. As the soloist completes the trill that usually closes the formal cadenza, the baton will give the preliminary beat and will rebound to the position from which the decisive attack-beat is to strike.

Leaving older classical examples, one occasionally finds cadenzas that introduce punctuating chords. As no measure-divisions or beat-divisions are set down or exist in these cases, the conductor can not outline divisions, as in the case of recitatives, but must merely rest until a chord-entry approaches. He then gives a quick preliminary beat and follows it with the attack-beat, quite as though he had been beating throughout. Usually however, there are structural features, even though measures are lacking, which forecast to the ears of the performers the attack into which the conductor presently leads them.

CHAPTER ELEVEN

The Left Hand, and Signaling

The left hand has important functions, but one point is clear: it should not become a mere additional right hand. At times, it is true, when all sections of large forces join in vigorous utterance, both hands may well pursue similar movements, may well "beat time" alike, and thereby almost double the animation and power of control. Usually, however, the left hand, if used at all, should perform distinct and separate duties.

As distinguished from those of the right hand, the duties of the left hand are generally more qualitative or expressional. Notwithstanding all that has been said about qualitative properties of beats, the prior duty of the right hand is metronomic. When its expressional indications are not sufficiently explicit, or are not sufficiently obeyed, the left hand adds its influence to them. For instance, a small beat by the right hand, growing smaller, may indicate a *diminuendo* that moves toward a *pianissimo;* but what conductor has not found it necessary in addition to hold a hushing left hand toward the performers. Palm down, in horizontal position or inclined slightly upward, and with sensitive fingers extended toward the too vigorous musicians, and perhaps stroking the tumult gently downward, it exerts a necessary subduing influence.

Control of dynamics is, indeed, one of the most important functions of the left hand. Palm upward, and with the addition of persuasive lifting movements, it stirs into fullness, prominence, confidence or power, tones that else would have failed to add their full weight of eloquence to the tonal address. Raised on high, and with fingers clenched, it energizes the performers to give "all they have" with power, decision, triumphant boldness. Outstretched, and with palm upraised and turned outward toward the performers, it warns, cautions, restrains: and it does this in infinite degrees, manifested by the inclination of the arm and the angle to which the hand is bent upward or downward, and by the reach of the arm, with respect to whether it is fully stretched out or is folded so as to bring the hand close to the body. The direction which the hand faces is, of course, determined by the location of the performer or performers so addressed. When large bodies are engaged in performance and the players or singers affected are remote, the outward reach of the arm, its elevation, and the inclination of the palm upward, are all likely to be quite marked. This is especially true if sudden and great subsidence in power is to be indicated; and in that case the gesture is likely to be commanding and comparatively abrupt. On the other hand, small subsidences and repressions that are sought in the interests of delicate balances of power are likely to be characterized either by a comparative lowering of the palm towards a horizontal position (palm downward) ; or by bringing it close to the body, although leaving it still upraised; or, in case the dynamic shadings to be dealt with are still more delicate, by combining nearness to the body with a less imperious position of the palm. The point to observe is that a vertical palm, turned to face directly a certain quarter, thrust outward to the full length of the arm, and elevated, represents the maximum possible to such a gesture of rejection, repudiation, and autocratic assertion. Turn the palm till it is oblique with respect to its object, relax it more or less from its vertical position, lower the arm, contract the arm and bring the hand nearer the body, and all sorts of other significances, together with all degrees of each, can be obtained. Gentle warning, friendly counsel to a little more restraint, persuasion that is confident of success or that is coldly exacting, may be intimated. The student would better investigate the range of possibilities, by some such plan as follows:

1. Begin with maximums with respect to (a) elevation of arm (which would be reached by a very slight inclination of the arm upward from the shoulder); (b) extension of arm; (c) uprightness of palm; (d) direct facing of palm.

2. Pass through successive modifications of (a) without modifying (b), (c), (d). *Note:* The conclusion will probably be that elevation of arm has largely to do with distance and elevation of performers, but that some degrees of peremptory quality, regardless of the position of the performers, nevertheless stand forth clearly.

3. Pass through successive modifications of (b) without modifying (a), (c), (d).

Note: The student will doubtless discover that this factor plays over a wide field of variations and is exceedingly eloquent.

4. Pass through successive modifications of (c) without modifying factors (a), (b), (d).

Note: The conclusion here is likely to be that this factor does not have a very wide range of play by itself: that is, relaxation of the palm from a vertical position is likely soon to be attended and reinforced by a lowering and a contracting of the arm, so far as momentary command is concerned. If indication of a continued *piano* or *pianissimo* is conceived as the problem, the importance of the effects attendant upon the position of the palm, with respect to its uprightness, will become much more evident.

5. Pass through successive modifications of (d) without modifying factors (a), (b), (c).

Note: Experiments here will probably prove that deflection of the palm changes the nature of the direction from a command to a signal, an invitation to join in, although some degrees of relaxation from power are also indicated. Also a tendency to change the palm from the vertical position, in company with its rotation toward oblique position, will be observed. The whole gesture readily connects with one that expresses encouragement and invitation to greater warmth and power.

6. Experiment with changes in two or more factors at once. An infinite variety is possible and infinite comment only could characterize them all. The action of the eyes, with respect to whether they turn to the point addressed by the hand and remain there with it or not, further increases the variety of effects.

It remains to be said that sometimes these indications by the left hand are accompanied by more or less rudimentary or complete beat-movements by the hand. If this beating achieves some purpose, and is consciously adopted as a part of his technique by the conductor, it is unobjectionable. Often, however, it is quite involuntary and subconscious and represents a lack of separate left-hand technique. The student may feel satisfied with his capability, with respect to this point, when he finds his left hand thoroughly independent and exhibiting no tendency to make rudimentary beats as a nervous reflex arising from the impulses given to the right hand.

Signaling

The word is often used but the act is seldom explained. The student accordingly feels that it represents a mysterious knowledge that some adepts somewhere must possess. It is really a quite simple matter with a technique that is far from being standardized.

Signaling has largely to do with the entry of parts that have been silent for a time, or that are to pick up some important thread of the composition after having been engaged with comparatively unimportant parts. The conductor is naturally concerned with their entry or their advance to the center of the stage, so to speak, and takes some care to prepare them for their moment of responsibility and give them confidence and support. The movements and indications by which he imparts such specifically directed information constitute his technique of signaling. While the form of it is by no means standardized and stereotyped, certain actions are almost inescapable and will almost invariably be followed by any conductor who has a good general technique and is deeply engrossed in faithfully delineating his music.

1. The conductor will, above all, turn his eyes toward the performers concerned and will catch their eyes.

Nothing proves ineptitude on the part of a conductor more convincingly than failure on his part to look toward and direct those performers who at the moment have important entries or musical responsibilities. The choral conductor who is inexperienced in orchestral work and who looks at the violins at the moment when a clarinet player is beginning a lovely solo part, not only is immediately rated by all who see and know as a poor conductor, but he does damage to the music because the clarinet player, being quite deserted and unable to grasp any intention from the wandering baton of his conductor, enters timidly, experimentally, and plays without authority. So one would speak to a person who heeded him not, but obviously was listening for remarks from another quarter.

2. The turn or glance toward the performers will precede their entry, or the crucial spot in their performance by a measure or by a beat or two. It is often accompanied by an uplift of the left hand: but in that case *the left hand should remain uplifted and quiet until the attack-beat arrives.*

A solo performer or a section of a group can no more make good entry upon one beat suddenly directed at them than could the entire chorus or orchestra so begin. Also it is true that a hand so lifted as a signal would better not descend unless and until a response is wanted.

3. The beats following the forecasting glance and possible lifting of the left hand may be directed elsewhere than to the signaled performers, but the last beat preceding the special entry should have in some degree the character of a phrasing-beat, in order to give decision to the entry-beat which follows. Usually the left hand, if raised, participates in this phrasing-beat or preliminary beat, by a slight movement upward, and then emphasizes the arrival of the crucial moment by falling as the baton strikes. This function of the left hand in signaling, as it has been described, is almost of as much value as its qualitative function, which was emphasized at length in the first part of the chapter.

———

In conclusion, know your music and while conducting live in and for your music. The proper movements will soon be acquired from that basis because they reflect musical conditions. It is far less certain that a technique acquired in a cold, rational frame of mind will lend itself flexibly to music.